Sing to Me

and

I Will

Hear You

Cover by Kelli Stohlmeyer, kelli@kel-i-design.com
Cover photo by Jan Born.

Elaine G. McGillicuddy
Sing to Me and I Will Hear You

Printed in the United States of America.
ISBN 978-0-9668228-8-5

Library of Congress Control Number: 2012938119

Caritas Communications
216 North Green Bay Road, Suite 208
Thiensville, Wisconsin 53092
dgawlik@wi.rr.com
414.531.0503

Sing to Me

and

I Will

Hear You

Elaine G. McGillicuddy

Caritas Communications   Thiensville, Wisconsin

For Francis
who knew how to
"surrender to Mystery."

LOVERS

Lovers, you who are for a while
sufficient to each other,
help me understand who we are.
Can we believe we endure?
You, however, who increase
through each other's delight,
you who ripen in each other's hands
like grapes in a vintage year:
I'm asking you
who we are.

You touch one another so reverently;
as though your caresses
could keep each place they cover
from disappearing.
As though, underneath, you could sense
that which will always exist.
So, as you embrace, you promise each other eternity.

From the "Second Duino Elegy"
Translated by Joanna Macy and Anita Barrows

Acknowledgements

I offer my deepest gratitude to the following: **David Gawlik,** my publisher - a photographer extraordinaire and longtime editor of *CORPUS REPORTS,* who upheld my earliest expressed wish to write Francis' and my story, yet cheered me on when it was poetry that came to me first, unexpectedly. **Bill Gregory,** a retired United Church of Christ minister whom Francis chose to help him "with the transition" and who has given me trusted guidance and support since Francis' death. He and his wife Nancy encouraged me as a poet, before I dared apply the word to myself. **April Ossmann,** poetry editor, from whom I sought a professional assessment after reading her article in *Poets & Writers.* Valuing the talent I hardly knew I had, she recognized my potential so encouraged me to publish my poems after seeking the services of a copy editor. **Mike O'Connor,** my reader, copy editor, and consultant - a poet, writer, publisher, and highly esteemed translator of Chinese literature (e.g., *Selected Poems of Chia Tao – When I Find You Again It Will Be In Mountains*) for saying, when he first read them, "I'm finding good things in the poems." As a result of his frankness, respect, good humor, and skill in alerting me where improvements were needed, and letting me make them myself, he became my on-the-job-poetry teacher. **Carolyn Barnwell,** a graduate of SALT Institute for Documentary Studies, who sought me as a subject for her radio story on the grief process. Her interview with me was fine enough to catch the ear of Seattle Public Radio producers who aired it. **Joanna Loehr,** a retired bio-chemistry professor, recently widowed, who, recognizing her own experience in that same SALT interview, took the initiative to make contact with me. As a new email friend, it was she who first showed my poems to **Mike O'Connor,**

Acknowledgements

her neighbor. **Barbara Briggs**, a retired librarian and member of our parish who reached out to me. Opening her gift of poetry books, I found another, a yet undiscovered gift of my own - to give words to my experience of grief and love through poetry. **Gloria Hutchinson**, a writer and longtime friend of Francis and mine, whose enthusiasm for my new commitment has never wavered. **Several friends** to whom I showed my poems in the beginning - as if to test - "Are they good enough to share?" helped by assuring me they were: Stephanie Abrams, Eugene Bianchi, Charlene Bickford, Jan Born, Peg Brown, Sally Chappell, De Ann Daigle, Barbara DeCoste, Denny Dreher, Donna Dyer, Nancy Earle, Sue Ewing, Sr. Anne Fitzpatrick, Melora Gregory, Eric and Hoa Herter, Anne Johnson, Brother Joseph Kilikevice, Joanna Leary, Caroline Loupe, Kathy Mills, Karen Hurll Montanaro, Allen Moore, Dr. Sheila Littlefield, Sandy Lucas, Emily Markides, Eleanor Morse, Bob Mottau, Tom Myers, Theresa Padovano, Marby Payson, Greg and Leona Phelan, Linda Pinto, Lori Power, Pat Proulx-Lough, Celeste Roberge, Dr. Joseph S. Roberts, Matthew Ryle, Mary and Dick Scaine, Annie Seikonia, Jennifer Stanbro, Kathy Tosney, Anne Underwood, and Sally Waite. I also thank **Sue Proulx** who urged me to make a CD of my reading the poems. Finally, I give heartfelt thanks to **Lynn Kuzma and Lee Slater**, parents of my goddaughter Rowan, who not only encouraged my poetry writing from the beginning, but recorded and made a CD of Francis' and my singing three chants shortly before Francis died. Their support of me has been unfailing, as if I actually am to them, mother and mother-in-law.

TABLE OF CONTENTS

TABLE OF CONTENTS

Preface

THE POEMS

Three books of poetry given to me by a friend nine months after my husband Francis died sparked something new in my life. The books were: Jane Kenyon's *The Book of Quiet Hours*, and especially her husband's - Donald Hall's *The Painted Bed* and *Without* in which he laments her death. Though a neophyte, inspired by a master poet - I got the idea: "I can do this." The sonnets I had written for my parents on their respective Mother's and Father's Day as a college freshman in 1953, hardly counted. Neither did those I wrote in the mid 90's about my struggles with a fibrous hip. Yet, encouraged by Hall's example, I turned to poetry to express my grief. I also wanted to preserve experiences Francis and I shared during the intense three months and ten days from the day his doctor told us "he has a cancer we don't know about" until he died on January 3, 2010.

The timing of these poetry book gifts was also significant in triggering my new muse: My letters to family and friends, beginning on September 24, 2009 keeping them informed about Francis' progress and ordeal, were posted on a blogspot one of my yoga students created for us www.elaineandfrancis. blogspot.com.

Since caring for Francis *at home* (Thank God!) took my full attention, I considered a few times cutting back on my detailed letters. A doctor friend told us: "Nerve bone pain from bone cancer is some of the worst pain known to humans." In addition to this challenge, Francis had diabetes. As his nurse, I was responsible not only for administering his medications and insulin shots, but for regularly changing his Fentanyl pain patches and watching over his TENS Unit and PCA (patient controlled analgesic) Dilaudid (morphine derivative) pump to which he was tethered 24-7. Its malfunctioning a few times raised our stress since his not always successful pain management plan depended on it.

Assistance in such occurrences was not as swift as promised since the hospice nurse on duty had to drive from out of town to reach us in the middle of the night. So temptation to write fewer, or only general updates, made sense.

But the English teacher in me felt compelled to record our passage together into the unknown. Doing so I unwittingly took everyone along with us, sharing not only the deeper journey, but also the bedside nitty-gritty details. As one hospice nurse related, "The first question we ask patients is: "How are your bowels and how is your nausea?" (I learned recently from a friend whose sister is dying that parts of my blog account were so helpful to their family, he printed them.) Since as it happened, friends thanked me for my frankness, I let go any remaining hesitancy to speak as candidly as is natural for me. The writing itself, moreover, seemed to give me strength, so I continued, even at the cost of sleep deprivation - for the sake of the story. Fully engaged day and some nights, I hardly had time to reflect on what I was communicating. But my readers did. That is why I decided to reread - with Francis at my side - the letters/blog I had written one year earlier, on September 24, 2009.

On September 24, 2010, one year to the day, I began reading what I had written then. As drawn to reenter the scene as a moth is attracted to light - sensing there was light in it for me even if it burned - I revisited and relived those experiences, and found healing in allowing as full a grieving as I was able to bear, at the time.

With the model of a grief-stricken poet to hearten me, the poems started coming. But none too soon since I needed strong arms on either side of me to support my great grief, even a year later.

THE STORY

With Francis' funeral over, several friends urged me to write our story, a request made several times in the past. After all, we lived interesting lives:

I, a former nun, at 37 married Francis, 45, who had been a Catholic diocesan priest. Without children of our own (we tried but failed to adopt an emotionally disturbed ten-year-old boy), we found other ways to generate offspring and a legacy.

In addition to our professions - I a teacher and Francis a Social Work Supervisor, we promoted peace as members of *Pax Christi*, and, for eight years, were conscientious war-tax objectors (http://www.paxchristimaine.org/).

Embarking on a lifelong practice of yoga in my 40's and Francis in his 50's, after returning from India, I co-directed for 16 years the studio we had co-founded (http://www.portlandyoga.com/whoweare.html). The following link includes a photograph of me teaching yoga at the Cumberland County Jail - Francis' ministry and mine for 11 years after teaching yoga to people with AIDS for five years: (http://www.portlandyoga.com/founders.html).

I continue to lead monthly circle "Dances of Universal Peace," in which Francis participated. As I do, he especially loved the Lord's Prayer and Beat-itudes chanted in Aramaic, and the Genesis story chanted in Hebrew, formed into sacred dances or body-prayers by Aramaic scholar Dr. Neil Douglas-Klotz. It is with that I began studying with him in 1996, after which Francis and I followed him to various states for yearly sacred dance retreats. This first is a link to a 14-minute You Tube video of "Saadi," as we call him (his Sufi name), leading us praying - with chant and movement - the first line of the Lord's Prayer. Francis and I are clearly in view as it begins:
(http://www.youtube.com/watch?v=J_mFa-B1wys);
(http://www.portlandyoga.com/dances.html) and,
(http://www.abwoon.com/shop/item.aspx?itemid=7).

Having worked with Francis for two years transforming our 8,000 square-foot lot into a demonstration site for permaculture, Francis and I held four Open Houses for neighbors and for our ever-expanding Portland Maine Per-maculture community. Any who wanted to, could come see and learn from our "Intro to Creating an Edible Suburban Ecosystem." This link to a folder of photographs taken on our property is only one of several folders of photos posted here: (http://www.meetup.com/portlandpermaculture/photos /211457).

Francis and I have also been longtime members of cta/usa, (http://www.cta-usa.org/) and of *CORPUS*. Since *CORPUS* members share our background as priests and in many, or most, cases as former nuns who married, the bonds we share with them are especially close knit. Their website includes a short arti-cle about us under "Chronicles from the Vineyard": (http://www.corpus.org/index.cfm?fuseaction=feature.display&feature_id=297). We attended, as I continue to do, yearly national conferences with both of these progressive Catholic communities.

Clearly, I had a lot to write about. But, while Francis was still living, I told friends - instead of writing about the past, I would prefer, as an elder, exploring areas of life I had until then barely cultivated, like the visual arts. Francis, for example, used his Portland Museum of Art pass much more than I, too engaged organizing and participating in our various community activities to make time for it. That was then.

Now, however, without Francis physically at my side, many reasons compel me. Shortly after Francis died, this idea appeared as a lifeline to me - a reason to go on living. Though still true, I realize now of course, there are many other compelling reasons besides this to go on living. What looms large is being a godmother to our seven-year-old goddaughter, Rowan. I want to bequeath our story to her. I also want to honor Francis, to unearth, or mine for myself, the riches of our life together, and share these with others, especially the love story. Bigger than both of us, the love is meant for all of us.

OUR DUET

So I will - in fact I have already begun to - write our story. Yet, when the poems kept coming, what else could I do but receive and offer them first?

The poems in this collection form one of an intended two-volume set of books, published separately. *Sing to Me and I Will Hear You – The Poems* is in your hands. When, as Providence allows, a second volume with an almost identical title appears - *Sing to Me and I Will Hear You – The Memoir: A Love Story*, I hope you will get that one too. It will include not only our story but, among other things, some love letters Francis wrote to me the summer after I left the convent, as well as selections from my journal after Francis' death.

IN THE MEANTIME

You're invited to read on (www.elaineandfrancis.blogspot.com) letters I wrote to family and friends, beginning on September 24, 2009 and continuing after Francis' death on January 3, 2010. These give accounts not only of his very well-attended funeral, but also of a special tree planting in the spring with many friends on our property, and an intimate "family" ceremony with Lynn, Lee, Rowan and me holding candles as I spoke and we sang - connecting with Francis by his tree in the snow on the first anniversary of his death. Here I also post new related developments, e.g., the date of publication of this book of Poems and its companion Memoir - perhaps soon, since I've taken a sabbatical from teaching yoga until it is completed.

Using the links on (www.elaineandfrancis.blogspot.com), you can also view two YouTube slideshows. Matthew Power, Editor of Liberty News TV, masterfully put together from our albums, choice photos that touch on all aspects of Francis' life. With three of our favorite musical selections as background, this photo slideshow is poignant.

So is the second YouTube slideshow created by Jan and Greg Born. Using his wife's photographs of Francis' wake, funeral, and reception, Greg, a whiz computer consultant, used as backdrop for the slideshow Francis' and my singing three chants recorded and made into a CD.

The first is "Set me as a seal upon your heart for love is as strong as death," from *Song of Songs 8:6*, and the second is the Beatitude of Jesus, in Aramaic, meaning: "Blessed are the pure in heart, those whose heart has a deep sense of passionate purpose and the audacity to feel abundant inside. They shall, in a flash of insight, see God everywhere." (Included here are both the traditional translation as well as Aramaic scholar Dr. Neil Douglas-Klotz' transliteration.)

The third chant, which accompanies these photographs, is Francis singing with me the whole Lord's Prayer in Aramaic. We had sung it together during the closing Liturgy at three annual *CORPUS* Conferences, one in Minnesota and two in Texas in June, 2008 and 2009. But when it was recorded 10 days before his death, we had no time to practice, so it was done spontaneously. What we hear on this recording is a very sick man singing with energy that audibly increases. Francis clearly took inspiration from the chants. Their revitalizing effect on him is demonstrated in a touching episode posted here on December 13, 2009: (http://elaineandfrancis.blogspot.com/2009/12/full-range-of-e-motions.html).

Using the following link posted on Feburary 18, 2011, you can listen to the eight-minute interview with me by Carolyn Barnwell, graduate of SALT Institute for Documentary Studies about my grieving process: (http://soundcloud.com/carolynbarnwell/sing-and-i-will-hear-you). It has been aired on several public radio stations since January 2011.

Looking back to when the poems started coming, nine months after Francis' death, it seems I could not bear allowing myself to feel the full loss of Francis' physical presence. I cried out in an early poem - "I could not bear the void ..." So I sought refuge as never before in fidelity to prayer. Still my mainstay, prayer, or as I prefer to call it - my sitting practice - is both balm and oasis to me. Many of the poems originated there, offering a glimpse into the progression of my journey through grief. And into love.

Note: A CD of my reading the poems in this collection is available from Caritas Communications which produced it, and Amazon.com, as well as from bookstores.

WHOOPEE

I was a nun and you, a priest.
We met in '68.
I left the Order in '70.
In 1971 the Rome debate
ended.
Vatican's Synod decreed:
no optional celibacy.

Confronted by authority,
you needed
a moratorium:
No calls, no visits,
no hope
for a married priest's ministry.
You anguished.
I wept
aloud.

But you wrestled with conscience, and
both of you won:
Deciding to leave the clergy,
you chose integrity.

Spotting an ad in a magazine
expressing your new resolve -
"On your mark,"
(it read beneath orchids in bloom)
"Get set, get ready, and grow!"
- you tore it out and

brought it to me exclaiming,
"I'm free!"
He could marry me!

I never got
more beautiful flowers
than those
which I framed,
penned with the date and your cry,
"Whoopee!"

38 years from that day
you died
in this room where it hangs -
your love proclamation:
to grow,
live fully,
and love.

WE MISSED ALL THE SIGNS

During gospels at church, you sat,
couldn't stand to join us at vigils,
were compelled to recline midday.

Many months, maybe years.
I sequenced yoga postures
to give you relief, and with
bodywork help, it worked!
So we stayed in the dark with the truth
lurking deep
in your bones.

Holding hands as I sat on your hospital bed
when the dread diagnosis
shocked us awake -
now we saw.
Now we knew.

And that look between us
held all
our mutual knowing and
loving regard of
41 years.

HOSPITAL WALK

It started out routine for her
when the physical therapist
fetched you from your room
for a walk down the long corridor.
But then you stopped.
You faced the rail,
curled firm both hands
around the bar,
straightened your arms,
and, bending your knees,
eased down your buttocks
for a yoga squat.

"It's yoga," you said, with a smile
She knew you were 82,
so she smiled too.

TWO FIRSTS

On your first-ever
radiation date,
no chair would do
for your pain-racked spine.

So you lay on a gurney
awaiting your turn,
with me looking on,
my face red, flushed
with hives.

To cheer us all -
"You know," I said - to the
therapists coming
to wheel you in -
"this man of mine,
20 years ago
at 62
kicked up
into his very first-ever
handstand."

POST-OP PREVIEW

I sat and I stood and
I sat again,
though I did slouch down
to rest a bit,
waiting for you
in the post-op room.

Too distracting to read
at a time like this.
Better be with my thoughts
and prayer.

I arose when the monitor
screen showed change,
eagerly squinting
to see your name
announcing you were ready
to return to your hospital room
and to me.

Though you smiled when you reached me
(you were wheeled on a gurney)
what I first saw
from a distance standing there
in the hall alone
(it was late) - was
your body lying still,
flanked by the surgeon and his help.

A post-op preview of that
awful sacred night
when they took away your body
in a shroud from our home.

SOME AFTERNOONS

you rose from your hospital bed
(the bed in our spacious living room
between the glass door facing the deck
into our garden next to the J-shaped chicken coop
and four tall windows fronting hemlock trees)
and slowly walked
through the room-wide threshold
to recline on our own bed mattress
lying on a custom-made frame
close to the floor.

Kneeling on the rug above your shoulders,
I would take into my hands
your long lean arms in mine and slowly
stretch them over your graying head.

You'd groan your pleasure
to feel your limbs alive,
your body's life still strong.

Your daily massage and these sensual
pleasures - all worth any effort of mine
as your personal nurse.

You were dying in the comfort of our home.

What You Say to Me

By now your spinal cancer pain
has chained you to your bed.
I floss your teeth;
I help you pee.
And what do you say to me?

"O what a wonderful moment this is!
My beloved's here with me.
You look good, you feel good,
and you are so good to me."
O Francis dear - What sweetness!
What love and brave acceptance!
You're forever seared upon my soul.

WHEN YOU FIRST BEGAN TO WITHDRAW

as the hospice booklet notes
that the dying do
many days ahead of time,
I instinctively knew
how to keep
the connection between us
flowing unimpeded (even now
beyond death):
I sought and held your mind with mine.

EARTHLY EXCHANGE

An artist's satisfaction -
his painting complete;
An infant's smile
responding to her mother;
A monk's grateful bow
accepting an offering;
A youth's anticipation
ready for adventure;
A bride and groom's gaze
exchanging their vows;
A runner's triumph.

These all - pale,
pale shadows of your radiant smile,
your luminous eyes
communicating to me
ineffable things,
your hands squeezing mine
and mine yours,
in our last
earthly exchange.

At Last

I could not live without you,
could not bear
the void.
Desperation spoke: "Just sit! Just sit."

I sat.
At last - communion.*

I came to sit with you, and
you came too.

*Communion of Saints: spiritual solidarity
of all God's people, living and dead.

PAIN'S SHARP EDGE

Pain's sharp edge
cuts through appearance
of disappearance.
Heart's remembering sharpens
sense to touch
new you, now, any when.

IN YOUR HEAVENLY PALACE

you could, now,
sink into bliss
all absorbing.

But you came to tryst with me,
your longing
as eager as mine.

You came.
You come,
my Bodhisattva.*

*In Buddhism, a bodhisattva is a
"wisdom-being," who, out of compassion,
delays entry into Nirvana
to help others achieve theirs.

BIG LOVE

You had died a few months before, and I was still sorely grieving,
trying to ease my pain, often late into the night, chanting consoling
Gregorian chants learned during 15 years as a nun.
I would sing those that expressed my prayer, like "Veni Sancte
Spiritus" - "Come, Holy Spirit, fill the hearts of your faithful, and
kindle in them the fire of your love."
One morning, some days later, after a visit to the chiropractor -

Remembering how you'd say,
"Drive carefully."
(revealing love's concern)
returning home one day
alone after you died,
my heart began to swell
with so much love
I was surprised,
so said out loud, still driving -
"It's big! It's BIG - YOUR LOVE!"

THE TANG

of your singular self
wakens my senses
to the joy of our lives
- so attuned to each other -
like a dance all these years,
its rhythm and beat pulses now in my life
with such force
I can feel both your hand and your step.

We're still moving together,
though the melody's new.

VISITATION

I first fell in love with your voice
on the convent telephone.
In the next 40 years as your wife,
it happened each time you called:
I loved you all over again.

At a peace demonstration, somewhere in the throng,
you coughed, and
I knew
it was you.
Many friends admired your rich handsome voice.

But I heard it again! Yes, Francis:
Even after you died, I heard it!
While making a grocery list,
(not even thinking of you,)
I palpably heard your voice!

The room did not hear - "I love you, dear,"
but my ears were filled with the un-
mistakable tone of your voice which
I heard!
It came clear. It came strong.
It was real.

May my tongue cleave to my palate if I do "forget"*
even just for a day -
your life-giving words
in your resonant voice.

*Psalm 137:6

DUET

I

"As death approaches me," you said at the end,
"even if I seem beyond your reach,
sing to me and I will hear you."
I sang. You heard.

Bereft of your voice after you died,
I turned to you with the same request:
"Sing to me, please - and I will hear you!"
You do. I hear.

II

Where did you go, my love?
I know you're not gone, not disappeared.
You live, you're alive! You're here!

The you who is here is the you transformed
as a seed in the earth dies to bear fruit.*
Descended into earth, the new you lives on!

When Great Mystery beckoned, you entered Her depths,
but left the door ajar for me.
Now I can hear you sing!

* John 12:24

ENOUGH

I know you know
I'm here, my love:
that is enough for me.
To be with you,
to know you know I'm here:
that is enough for me.

INTACT

You come,
not as ghostly airy spirit,
but all intact;
freckly self's crannies and nooks
known to me alone;
intact as essence distilled,
as marrow, as substance, as core,
nectar,
ambrosia of you
for me to drink.

REMINDERS

Your place in our bed beside me,
Your chair near our kitchen stove,
Your sweater that keeps me warm,
Your writing on a recipe card,
Your shoulder-bag hung on a hook,
My new prayer shawl -
the shroud that wrapped your body.

These reminders,
and hundreds still, all around town,
bring me stabs of pain.
But even more - your caressing touch.

ABSENT ABSENCE

Your presence with me now
my love is
stronger in your absence
than fleshly presence then.

Our Bed

I

Your pillow lies alone, near mine.
It numbs me to remember -
one year ago today,*
you slept in our bed
for the last
time.

II

But I remember too: This bed's where
our *"petits cris de joie"*^ arose
in our early years - where
I, night person, finally crawled in
and spoon-shaped myself to you - where
after nine weeks away in India,
I slept on you nightlong - where
we hugged and held to express our love,
after health problems slowed you down.

You often said, off to bed, you'd be
"plugging into the infinite."

I'm plugging in too, to be with you
every night in our bed.

* 9/24/09
^ "little cries of joy" as my
uncle joked.

MEMORY THREADS

Each memory thread of you
doesn't tie me to the past, but
continues to create
this tapestry
I'm weaving now.

WISH BONE

Early-bird Francis, you met early-bird chickens
each morning
before your bone pain deepened.

Back from the bathroom en route to bed,
I peek outside from our deck's glass door
to watch you in the chicken pen
peering through the coop pop-door
just unlocked -
sweet clucking hens
rushing out between your legs.

For the chickens' sake,
come Francis, my saint,
reset my clock circadian to yours.
I want to be an early bird, too.

My Home

"You're in my central core
and I'm in yours,"
you wrote when first we fell in this unending love.

Did you know then He said it first? -
"Abide in me and I in you."*

No matter now,
I have a home.

*John 15:4

HOME TO ONE ANOTHER

One day after you died,
we walked into each other,
and lingered
there
a while.

Another time in church,
from where you used to stand
beside me,
you stepped into my space so that
I stood within you
enveloped by your taller frame.

Then all at once I understood
anew
your lover's words (our early bliss):
"You're in my central core
and I'm in yours."

Words now flesh beyond the grave.

THIS NEW LIFE

It suits me for now -
this new life with you
God-deep in your Love-merged heart
holding me,
while I walk through . . . now live fuller . . . my days;
you, in this new life with me.

Pepere Is God

I knew the ancient joy we humans feel in sharing like experience
when I read *A Grief Observed*. Here C.S. Lewis invites us
to love "not any image, or memory" of the dead,
but to love them in their wondrous reality.
However, since "this is not now imaginable," he explains,
"the dead are like God. In that respect, loving (them) has become…
like loving Him." p. 78

But another joy awaited me:

"Pepere is God," Rowan announced
emphatically,
twice,
one week apart,
six months after you died.

"God-daughter, dear,"
(She was six-years old)
"not quite."

But then I remembered the passage
and marveled.

ELEVEN MONTHS LATER

Never again our white Toyota
rounding the bend of our Avalon Road
-   you, coming home to me.
Never again your dark handsome head
peeking through our kitchen window
-   you, hugging grocery bags for us.

I Had To

I had to find you in my soul
before I could bear the weight of my crushing loss.

I had to hear you in my heart
before I could face the loss of your resonant voice.

I had to feel the warmth of your transforming presence
before I could withstand the cold of your bodily absence.

I had to sit with you in prayer
before I could tolerate your empty chair.

I had to taste the sweetness of your comfort
before I could drink the bitter cup of grief.

I had to touch with you your heavenly peace
before I could let you go.

I had to find the light of you for my path
before I could see and walk in the dark.

I had to feel the ardor of This Love that never dies
before I could agree: Love is stronger than death.*

*Song of Songs 8:6

UNBIDDEN

What earthly lover could reciprocate
as only you now do?
Unencumbered by your body,
you abide in me, and I in you.

When standing in a postal line,
or stalled in our car for a passing train.
I call, and you come
to accompany me.

When unaware
I'm in need of your advice,
you come unbidden
to touch my soul at will,
and I lack nothing.*

*Psalm 23:1

You Gave Me No Clue

I'd encounter you
at the annual King celebration.*
I wasn't in grief -
How could I be?
You came to accompany me!

You weren't left out,
I found that out:
surrounded by friends at our table,
friends who met yearly for this –
between speakers, awards, and
the dinner itself -
I sensed in my gladness and
laughter a joy
too expansive, too deep
to have come from myself
alone.

No - I knew it was you enjoying
our friends by
living my life with me.

*Martin Luther King NAACP Dinner

PHYSICAL FLIPS AFTER YOUR DEATH

Why does this photo of you
in your winter blue pajamas
physically flip my heart?

Your aging handsome face?
The twinkling of your eyes?
The gesture of your love –
puckering your lips
to offer me a kiss?

Yes, love, it's the love –
in your face, in your eyes, in your smile
that enlivens my heart and my life.
It's your love.

ANYWHERE

No need to get home
to be with you -
I carry home with me.
So I'll just relax
and enjoy to the max
your anywhere moment with me.

FRIENDS

Widows need powerful friends
with influence in many spheres.

My friend, Intention, with her speed of thought,
telepathically touches you.

Memory's stories, with her nose for detail and
her sensory perceptions,
comfort and cheer me as she keeps in touch
with the you I knew.

But Faith presents me with
Love's House of Prayer* which
holds you fast
in my soul.

*I Thessalonians 5:17

COME FOR A WALK WITH ME

On the trail to the cemetery,
surprises abound - the
fox with her pups
and the heron in the pond
giving study to the frog.

Here our bodies relax as
we walk,
watching birds flying free
in the sky's blue expanse
where the trees' canopies
circle round the headstones
red with sun
setting down.

Here I come
for a walk with you.
Here - surprises
abound.

HOKMAH'S ADVICE

My mother Hokmah counseled me:
Make time for your sister, Solitude;
Go tryst with your beloved, Intimacy;
Join in with your friends, Community.
My mother lives up to her name.

* "Hokmah" in Hebrew means "wisdom."

THE SWEETEST YET

The fruits of this love
we nurtured together
are ripe for the picking.
Their sweetness this season
of our seeming separation
exceed any flavor we savored before.

I Need to Touch

every day
the flesh of your spirit
I call presence.

It's that touch,
indispensable,
that gives me
the will to go on.

Without it, I'd be
a stranger to myself -
lost to the world.

THERE IS MORE

Not just to survive
by assuring myself I'm deeply loved,
so have nothing more to fear,
but also, I come to you too - to celebrate
your grace
I didn't fully see before, and
to be present with you before
the Mystery unfolding
brightly before your eyes,
and darkly before my own.*

*I Corinthians 13:12

ONE DAY

I sat quietly in prayer,
chanted our two songs,
freed the chickens from the coop,
worked in our garden,
helped out at the pantry,
prepared for my class,
caught up on some reading,
closed the chickens' pop door,
joined a friend at the theater . . .

And then, my dear –
I entered the house
of our Love.

More Than Dream

Why did you come in a dream
more substantial than daylight?
We held and we knew we were here.

Nothing now holds you back.
Without ears I can hear you, and
see for myself without eyes.

To reach you I walk on water,
fly to your side, and -
without hands of my own -
hold yours.

GOD WITH YOUR FLAVOR

A holy Sufi*
said
we're like layers of an onion.
Peel them all away and there's
nothing at the core
but God.

As it is with you,
I can hardly take it in:
God, with your flavor?
But I'll savor
God as you for now.

        *Sufi Shaykh ad-Darqaw

YOUR POETIC SOUL

Two days before you died,
you discovered yourself anew:
"I never thought myself a poet,"
you said.
"But I have a poetic soul.
It steered me through
a lot of decisions."

O Francis, - yes! But there's more:
At 43, young lover,
you told me my core was in yours, and
yours in mine.

And on your deathbed, this at 82 -
"Your presence was deeply
drawn into my soul."

Painful Birth

Papa's death - heart torqued with grief;
Maman's death - elemental wrenching
at the root;
Francis' death - ripped out of myself,
uprooted, transplanted to
new-dimensional worlds.

WHOEVER HEARD

a more loving
request of his wife
by a dying man - to
accompany you
by singing alone
our love-vow chant
as you passed?

Oh, my love, not "request" -
but your gift to me.

Whoever heard an
answer like this when the
hospice nurse asked you:
"What's holding you back?"
"It's the joy," you said.

Oh Francis, this joy
in our love beyond death
holds me here daily in prayer.

Nothing Can Fill

this gargantuan gaping
hole of my loss -

except this:

my relief at sparing you
a widower's pain.

SPRINGING UP DEEP

    from its Source where you live:
    the Love-drink you offer
    that quenches my thirst.
    To whom else should I go?*

                * John 6:68

FOR TWO DAYS

I spent time with our families and us
choosing photos from our albums for this book.

All our lives - and the lives of friends
who have passed - spread out there
on the dining room table . . .
in our gardens, at our jobs, painting rooms.
All those gatherings, activities, and trips
ended now.

Impermanence
with a face.

I went for a walk and remembered
how after you died someone told me -
"It'll take you two years.
Yes, two."

I'm lacking five months, and
I forget whom he was who predicted,
but I know that he knew, since

I never before
looked out of these eyes
- my expressionless face -
as if dazed from a blow,
like this.

WIDOW'S TIME

My widow's time is moving time,
not moving on, but in.
Let self inhabit new-found rooms
reserved beforehand for me.

My widow's time is harvest time.
Let love crack open
memories' nuts
yielding their sweet meats.

My widow's time is wisdom time.
Let me embody
lessons learned –
my legacy to youth.

My widow's time is midwife time.
All creation groans,*
so let me serve in
restoration of the earth.

*Romans 8:22

LIKE A TIDE

Your presence lives
in this sea of silence here,
still our home, and
the island of my soul.
But a tide draws me out -
in ebb and flow -
to play with the children and
work with the lovers and elders
who long for a planet restored.

ON FIRE WITH YOU

Matter is frozen light given
birth as sparks of the Original Shining. So
every person bears, in
each one's bones, the stuff of stars.

When we - like twin stars - wed, we
brightly shone as one. But
death ignited your spark into the
Blaze of Love's Own Fire.

When we wed, we sensed but dimly the
grandeur of our final consummation
- when I will be with you
on fire with Love.

Recognizing

in its sweetness
a telltale sign
of your presence –
already here
within and around me –
I hasten with an embrace
and rest in it with you.

At Home, on My Way Home at 75

This Eden earth is alive to me:
A buzzing bee, a trilling frog,
the joy of a child at play;
a baby's birth, a husband's death,
humanity's struggle for peace.

But the child of my longing
reaches out as deep and far
as the Universe
steeped in Spirit Space
my second home
where I belong
for unending discovery
with all Beloveds.

ON THIS FRESH SUMMER MORNING

squatting by these bushes
we planted here together
before you died,
I pluck plump blueberries and
eat them on the spot.

Your graceful tree's behind me -
a Japanese stewartia,
nourished by your ashes.

Planted by our friends
it stands
not in memory alone, but as
symbol: Love that lasts.

The calls of chickadees and crickets,
the seamless chant of locusts and cicadas
(soul-stirring since my youth),
move me to discover you
my breakfast company.

How Can It Be

- even more than Jesus -
I'm finding you here for me?

Of course, it's He in you,
but because I hear your voice,
remembering what you'd say,
your compassion
wraps me round
repeatedly
and eases my way.

LIKE THE GROUND

beneath my feet,
garden earth,
hardwood floor,
rug in our cosy
living room -
even the asphalt on
my daily walk;

Like the breath that
never leaves me,
swelling with joy as
I harvest grapes,
rising and falling in
my trusting sleep -
even instrumental
in calming distress;

Like the water we'd
die without,
slaking our thirst
when we're feeling dry,
benefits our bodies
needing a bath -
even just for pleasure
taking a swim;

Like the food
we need to live,
firing up energy
so muscles work.
giving us nourishment,
vigor to live -
even as dessert,
foretaste of heaven:

Your presence is my ground,
my breath, my water,
my food.

HE STOOD ON OUR LADDER

picking peaches while I
gathered those fallen on the ground.
This African youth
I hired to help me
broke out
now and then in song.

I learned in the kitchen,
trimming our peaches,
he'd fled his country, Burundi,
for fear of his life:
his father was poisoned;
his mother died young.

After dropping him off -
my new young friend -
and while driving back home,
I wondered, dear Francis:

As I grow into widening
worlds of experience,
listening to stories like this,
through your loving communion with me -
do you grow too?
I ask, since
now at The Source,
what else could you possibly gain?

Yet remembering
this Wellspring, our God, counts
"the very hairs on (our) heads,"*
I know
that you grow when I do.

* Luke 12:7

I Hear You Francis

Let me learn and live the
wisdom revealed in
these last words of yours:

"I feel so good. So good!
I don't know
which step this is
along the way.
No, I don't know.

But whatever step it is,
I embrace it.
I do embrace it."

POSTSCRIPT TO THE POEMS: A PAGE FROM MY JOURNAL

The poems are ready for the publisher. I like ending the book with Francis' words. They apply to all of us; like him, not knowing what our next step will be, we can keep ourselves in a state of readiness to embrace it.

Who knows my next step? At my age I've learned life is full of surprising turns. I wrote the author biography yesterday: "McGillicuddy lives a largely monastic life at home in Portland."

This is the first time, since Francis' death about 21 months ago, that I publicly expressed what I've discovered suits me. This monastic life (prayer, study, work, and recreation) is a treasure, a pearl of great price I should not easily give up - not only for my own sake, since it provides what my heart has longed for all my life, revealed by entering the convent in 1954; being drawn into yoga in 1978; going to India to study yoga in 1989 - but also because living close to the Source where the waters run deep, I can draw up drink to share with others.

Is this being pretentious? I'll let the providential universe decide, letting myself be guided by *wu-wei*, what I learned years ago from master yoga teacher, Dona Holleman and her book *Centering Down*. I quoted it then for my yoga students: *Wu-wei*, as emphasized by the Taoist school of Chinese thought, aims for alignment with the Tao - without effort.

Yes, this deep place is where I find myself, as well as find Francis. It does "suit me for now - / this new life" with you / God-deep in your Love-merged heart / holding me, / while I walk through . . . now live fuller . . . my days; / you, in this new life with me."

And yes, "My widow's time is moving time, / not moving on, but in. / Let self inhabit new found rooms / reserved beforehand for me."

Yes, yes, these poems - given me to work with - are my guide now too. Their truth resounds like a bell that calls me through the clouds and darkness and storms that come with life on this plane. They are like a map drawn up specifically for me, painstakingly sketched by the Cartographer. They're custom-made. Ah, there's a poem here!

THESE POEMS

- custom-made maps
carefully drawn
by the Cartographer
offering to show me
my way.

These poems
- like bells ringing out
my truth, resounding
through the clouds and
darkness, guide
me home.

Written September 25, 2011 - my 76th birthday

AT THE TEMPLE CEREMONY FOR THE DEPARTED DAUGHTER

Unbearable grief.
For not so brief an instant
as that between the notes
of the monks' bell
will I forget you.

Izuma Shikibu, Japanese poet (11th Century)
Translated by Steve Kowit

Elaine G. McGillicuddy, a native Mainer, is a retired high school English teacher. She lived in Missouri, New York, Massachusetts, and Waterville, Maine, during the 15½ years that she was an Ursuline nun. In 1968, while Campus Minister at Colby College, she met and later married Francis A. McGillicuddy after he left the clerical priesthood. She has a B.A. in English from the College of New Rochelle, New York, an M.A. in Religious Studies from Providence College, Rhode island, and is a certified Iyengar Yoga teacher, leader of the Dances of Universal Peace, and permaculture designer. Widowed in 2010, McGillicuddy lives a largely monastic life at home in Portland Maine.

While working on her next book, *Sing to Me and I Will Hear You - The Memoir: A Love Story,* she is on sabbatical from teaching her weekly yoga class at Portland Yoga Studio, which she co-founded with Francis in 1989. This is her first collection of poetry.